Discovering, Defining & Defeating…

THE FIEND

By: Zachary Mitchell

Published by Unbreakable Publishing
Clarissa L. Green, Editor-in-Chief

Disclaimer: Some names of people, businesses and identifying details have been altered to protect the privacy of others.

This book is not an evidence-based approach to drug addiction treatment and has not been approved or certified by any federal, state or local agency/facility programs.

First printing November 2017
Written by Zachary Mitchell

Edited by Clarissa L. Green
Cover Photo Designed by: Steven Garner

Published by Unbreakable Publishing Company, LLC
Milwaukee, WI

Discovering, Defining & Defeating…

THE FIEND

By: Zachary Mitchell
Author of Road to Damascus

Zachary Mitchell

DEDICATION

This book is dedicated to my "soldiers" Zachary Mychal & Z.J. Your futures mean so much to me. Also to my brothers and sisters out there fighting this fight...**We Can Win**!

-Zachary Mitchell

Fear not, for I am with you; be not dismayed, for I am your God; I will strengthen you, I will help you, I will uphold you with my righteous right hand.

Isaiah 41:10

CONTENTS

Zachary Mitchell

ACKNOWLEDGMENTS

I would first like to acknowledge my creator: my Lord & Savior Jesus Christ. If it had not been for Him, let me tell you, I would NOT be here!

Next, I would like to acknowledge my parole officer: Susan Wundrow. She has had such a profound impact on my life. Make no mistake, she is "no nonsense" and will do her job, but she also believes in the success of her clients and I'm a grateful recipient of that support.

I would also like to acknowledge my church family. They rode the wave of adversity with me for three years. I've received unconditional love from them! To Jim & Marv: thanks for being an example of Godly manhood!

I would like to acknowledge the Wisconsin and Upper Michigan Division of the Salvation Army. They've been examples of "laborers of love". I thank God for you all.

To my Milwaukee Citadel family, Majors Gary & Donna, Karen & Keisha, Candy, Chenon, the children and church family: You guys just don't understand the love I have for you all for what you loved me through. Samantha Jones(Nolan)...you already know!

Next up, to Rich, Ree, Frank & LaDawn Woods, Bobby Sunday, Sharon, Cristina, WreckTown, C.F.L, Curt, Lavoris- my Captive Project Fam: One word, WOW! Thanks for the prayers and walking with me through everything! Love also to the extension- Al & Ro, "Sons of Faith": Love you as well brothers!

I want to acknowledge Ms. "P" from the Relapse Prevention Program at M.S.D.F. for really connecting some loose threads for me. Also to Fred, Scott, A.J, J.D, Renteria, Knnack, Anderson, Brandon, Krenke, Cristova, Zimmerman, Bobby, Matt, Mr. Foster and the rest of the guys on 5C.

Perry Brown, Ashley Thomas from Hope Street: Thanks for

viii

giving me that 3rd shot! To my Hope Street Fam- Myra, Sheila, Bill, Charles, Eli, Tamikur, Tisha, and everyone else: LOVE!

Nicole Pryor, thanks for hearing my mind! Shekina...You already know! To "Room #402" of the A.R.C- Rick, Josh, Chico, my bro Trevor Sumner: Much love family! Oh, can't forget "The Kracken", Jordan!

To Jerry, J.B., Marvin, Eric Kirby, Andy Kramer, Antwan, Johnny R., Brad, Jason, Mr. Epps, Capts, Jeremy Steinke and the rest of the fellas at the A.R.C.

Wow, there are plenty more that prayed for me! To my sisters Evelyn, Evett & Rachel and my brothers Reggie & Marshaundus. To J. Bentley, Daniel "D'Aych" Harris, & Markasa Tucker: LOVE!!

Momma Norma, Pastor Fair, Momma Beverly, Elder Starr, Mike & Sis. Bev, the whole St. James Community Mission Church fam: Much Love!

I also want to acknowledge a kind, compassionate friend who came and saw me at my worst & bought me lunch (with Jada's approval- inside joke): Irie". "I want to acknowledge Chaney, I thank you for your oftentimes TOUGH LOVE, but also being a steady friend."

I definitely want to acknowledge Bro. Brian of the Andrew Ministry of Christ The King Church for the powerful teachings down at M.S.D.F. You are a TRUE servant of our Lord!

Last but DEFINITELY not least: UNBREAKABLE PUBLISHING! Thank you for believing in this project and lending your gift & expertise in making it a reality!

To the men/women who draw the strength to pick this book up: you are stronger than you think! Much love on your road to redemption!

HISTORY

For many years, it has been believed that the United States government had a conspiracy to kill off the African American race.

One of the most talked about conspiracy theories was the crack epidemic.

In the mid-80's and early 90's it is believed that the government flooded the black communities with crack cocaine.

Cocaine, also known as coke, is a strong stimulant used as a recreational drug made from a Coca leaf. Common ways of usage are snorting, inhaling or injecting into the veins.

Per Wikipedia, the free encyclopedia, mental effects of cocaine usage include loss of contact with reality, an intense feeling of happiness or agitation. Physical symptoms may include faster heart rate, sweating and large pupils. Effects begin within seconds to minutes of use and last between five and ninety minutes.

Cocaine was eventually converted into rock form, known as crack rock[1] and sold in smaller quantities. This made it easier to produce and was highly profitable for drug dealers.

---

[1] A solid, smokable form of cocaine

The biggest impact of the crack epidemic were large areas in the United States such as Los Angeles & San Diego, CA, Houston, TX, Miami, FL and in the Caribbean.

Introduction

A long time ago, I took a certification course in horticulture. Horticulture is the art or practice of garden cultivation and management. It includes the cultivation of medical plants, flowers, fruits, vegetables, nuts, and more.

I learned that in order to treat different problems or diseases that occur in plants, you may have to check the rooting system. On the surface of a wilting plant, you could perform certain treatments that would sustain them for a while. However, if there is a root issue that's not detected, they will eventually wilt and die.

My theory is that a "root issue" principle is abstract in the treatment of chemical dependency. Chemical dependency is the addiction to a mood or mind-altering drug such as alcohol or cocaine.

As an ex-addict to cocaine for over twenty years, I've been in countless detox and sobriety programs and a member of numerous support groups. I couldn't understand why I seemed to be on sort of a slippery slope in relation to my recovery.

It wasn't until the year 2012 that I realized that due to my reluctance to address the root[2] causes of why I chose to use

---

[2] An understanding of the causes or basis of a problem

drugs as a "cosmetic treatment" in my recovery, this was the very reason I hadn't sustained sobriety.

I'm sure many can agree with me on this thought process. There are men and women who are sick and tired, busted and disgusted, who's sincere about digging through the diseased soil of past hurt and other issues that led to a life of false peace.

I had in mind that an individual or group could use my past experiences, as a gardener would use a spade, to dig up all impediments that may be in the way of getting to the root causes of their own issues or habits.

I've come to the realization that the roots of my childhood and early adulthood, affected my life tremendously in relation to the continuous drug use.

My childhood wasn't the worse but like everyone else, it had some impurities and imperfections.

I was born in Milwaukee and moved to South Bend, IN around the age of three with my mother and father. We bounced around for some time and eventually settled in San Francisco, CA. Things took a turn for the worse when a deep, dark family secret came to light and crushed my whole world.

The Beginning: *Discovering*

Iconic Hip Hop Artist Ice Cube voice boomed from the speakers of a car passing as I walked pass the recreation center in the Lakeview neighborhood of San Francisco, CA on my way to work. I was enraptured by the material trappings of the hood life at that time.

I didn't run the streets or engage in criminal activity. In fact, I attended a religious boarding school a few hours away from San Francisco.

One day I got into a fight with another student and was discharged from school. When my uncle picked me up from the bus station, he broke down some shattering news to me.

My uncle told me that my family, which consisted of my parents, my three younger brothers and my baby sister, left town and moved to the Midwest. How could they just up and leave me like that?

On top of that, I got the devastating news that the only man I knew as dad, was not my biological father. I was devastated! I felt unloved, neglected and was put in a bad place mentally.

My uncle allowed me to stay with him and his family. My cousin and I were the same age, so we grew a tight-knit.

Being around the ages of sixteen and seventeen, me, my cousin, and our friends spent most of our time at different church events or playing basketball.

We weren't bad kids, but we had our times of mischief. We'd get caught trying to do small things such as breaking curfew, petty theft or sneaking out the house after being told to stay in.

One day, one of our buddies told us that he started selling drugs with one of the neighborhood dealers. It went well for a couple weeks until one night the Task Force Unit beat him up for running from them. Once he explained it to his parents, it was a wrap for his business.

My cousin and I went to visit him at his house. We laughed and joked as he told us the story about his little fiasco. But behind the laughter, I became curious of trying to sell drugs myself.

With the situations I encountered at home, I had become sort of a chameleon. To escape from these realities, I wanted to be like anyone rather than being myself. Plus, like a bunch of guys my age, I wanted to dress like the hustlers or drug dealers.

They drove the fancy luxury cars, wore the latest fashion, and had expensive jewelry. Not to mention the things that comes with lots of money; power and easy access to beautiful women!

One day I took the few dollars I had in my pocket along with a semi-expensive watch I had on my wrist and went around the block to the recreation center.

The rec center was a popular hang-out spot in the neighborhood. There was lots of known gang activity, drug dealing, and gambling near the center. You were bound to get some sort of connect with just about any type of illegal activity at the center.

I asked a guy standing outside if he knew anyone who wanted to buy the watch. Seeing him out there regularly as I walked to my uncle's house from work, I knew he had some sort of ties to the illegal activities or knew someone who did. Little did I know the guy was a drug user.

He asked a few questions about my intent with the money so he could get me the best price. He told me he knew who to go to, to get rid of it for me. He left for about fifteen minutes and came back with some cash.

He told me he could get me a nice amount of dope[3] for the money I had. Since I was a rookie, he told me he would help me out once he purchased some. He showed me how to weigh it, how to bag it, how much to sell it for and what approaches to use to get me a sale.

After selling a few rocks[4], the guy tells me he knows a spot[5] up the street we could possibly make more money.

We went in, he stepped in the bathroom and talks with the lady. He came out and told me that she wanted to talk to me.

I went in and asked her what she needed. She asked if she could have a taste[6] to see if my product was any good. I gave her a sample. She hits it, licks her lips, then tells me she didn't have any money now but was expecting some soon.

I was stunned at what I was witnessing! I'd watch movies with

---

[3] A drug taken illegally for recreational purposes

[4] Small and rock-shaped single serving of crack cocaine

[5] Street term for place used to conduct drug transactions

[6] To sample a tiny amount of substance from a cocaine rock to test its purity which increase the strength of the numbness

drug use but never saw someone use drugs with my own two eyes besides smoking marijuana for recreational use. On-looking something so extreme had me bamboozled!

She asked if she could exchange some sexual favors for a bigger sized rock. I looked her up and down, checking out her tempting body physique and agreed.

I gave her the rock, she takes a piece, puts it on the pipe then says we could really get freaky if I took a hit with her. I told her that I didn't use drugs, I was just a dealer. She takes another hit then starts undressing. I started undressing too. Again, she tries to convince me to take a hit. I emphatically told her that I didn't use. We took care of our quick sexual encounter and I left out the bathroom.

I told the guy I was with that she didn't have money. I'm sure he knew that, he just wanted to help her get what she wanted. Before we could get out the door, she comes out the bathroom asking if she could exchange additional sexual favors for some beer and cigarettes. I declined the favor but gave her a couple dollars for the smokes and drink anyway.

This was my first encounter as a drug dealer. I couldn't believe that my first deal was a dope-date[7]. Then I turned around and gave her some of my money when I hadn't even made a profit yet.

After a couple hours hanging around the neighborhood, my guy says it will be too dangerous now that it was getting dark. This was a tough neighborhood and we would easily be targeted as robbery victims out here selling drugs.

He told me he had a sister in the projects where we could chill[8]

---

[7] Sexual favor provided by a drug user in exchange for drugs/dope

[8] Relax or wait around

and get customers to make more money.
We made our way to her house. When I saw this woman, I was instantly attracted. My guy asked her, just like he did before, to speak to him in the other room. He comes out and tells me that she was okay with us staying over for a while. He said that he'd be back in a few, he had to go get some food and drinks.

A few minutes after he left, his sister came out with an alluring lingerie piece that made me almost jump out of my skin! Right away I ask what she wanted to do. She said she didn't party unless both parties participated. I said I didn't get down like that. She said cool. She asked if she could get a rock, it was her spot after all. So, I gave it to her.

After she took a hit, she stood up started dancing slowly saying how good it was. I told her that there was more where that came from! She, just like the other lady, invited me to join her. I told her that I would pass.

She walked over and looked out the window. She knew I was turned on and smiled at me looking over her shoulder. I gave in and told her to come on! Her sex appeal tempted me, and she ultimately persuaded me to smoke with her.

It seemed as if my guy just magically appeared just as things started getting fun! I ended it there and left with him. Surprisingly, I didn't get addicted.

Two years later, back in the Midwest in Milwaukee, WI, was my next encounter using drugs when I was in a relationship with an older woman.

Her son, who was just two years younger than I was, found a drug pack someone dropped near an alleyway near her friend's house. I convinced him to let me have it to sell it. I told him that I would split the profit with him.

I had every intention to do just that until I told his auntie what we came across. I met her and her brother at an apartment and ended up partying with them. We smoked continuously the entire night. I didn't make a single dollar from it.

After my first experience of continuous drug use, luckily, I didn't get addicted then either. Now that I had two episodes with drug use and wasn't addicted, I began to believe that it was "mind over matter". I deemed that a person who let themselves become a hype[9] or an addict, wanted to be one.

But then the fall of 1991 came. I was 21, a newlywed with a baby girl, and my wife was pregnant with my first-born son. The baby girl was not mines biologically but I didn't treat her or love her any different than my first-born child.

One day a longtime friend stopped by. He was emotional because his father had just passed. I knew his father personally, so it hurt me as well. Assuring him that I'd be there for him during his time of need, I asked was there anything I could do.

He asked if I could loan him some money to buy some drugs to take the edge off. I originally thought he was talking about smoking weed[10]. He ultimately told me he was talking about cocaine. I never knew him to do anything, but smoke weed and drink.

Milwaukee only sold powder cocaine at that time. When we got the drugs, enough for both of us, he told me he was rocking his up. Since I knew I couldn't get hooked, I went ahead and smoked with him.

It was the beginning of the end!

---

[9] An extreme drug user

[10] Street term for marijuana

<u>DISCUSSION QUESTIONS</u>

Reflect back to the first encounter around your substance of choice. Discuss the first time you used your substance of choice.

1. What circumstance put you in position to be in the presence of the substance?
2. Prior to your use, what were you experiencing emotionally? Financially? Mentally? Physically?
3. What led to your first encounter or usage?
4. Discuss whether you were coerced or just experimenting?

_____
_____
_____
_____
_____
_____
_____
_____
_____
_____
_____
_____
_____
_____
_____
_____
_____
_____
_____
_____
_____

The Middle: Defining

The last use while grieving with my friend started an avalanche of heartache and trouble in my life. It was no longer "mind over matter" for me. I was hooked and there was no denying it! I spent all the money I got my hands on towards drugs and used multiple times a day. After each use, I used some more, all the while yearning for that immaculate high[11] as before.

For a while, I told my wife that I was losing our money gambling. All along, her woman intuition knew that was a lie. So many things were recognizable, yet I remained oblivious as if she was clueless.

She moved to the city of Milwaukee to be with me after meeting when I moved to her hometown some years back. The place we stayed was unfamiliar to her. She had no family, very few friends and me. I'd leave her home alone all day and night. Here she was, isolated in a new city, pregnant, going to doctor's appointments alone, while I ran the streets getting high.

Then she caught me red-handed! One day, she found a pipe in my jacket pocket. Another time, she undressed me when I went to sleep and discovered I had been unfaithful. The evidence of

---

[11] The feeling resulting from chemical buildup between nerves causes such a euphoria

sexual activity was on my underwear.

She eventually got fed up with my shenanigans and left me. She called her mom to pick her and her belongings up.

When she left, I used more frequently and cared less about my responsibilities. I allowed a couple dope dealers to use my apartment as a spot or drug house. I now had easy access to free dope! This led to numerous all-nighters using drugs.

A few months later, after talking with my estranged wife and her step father, I felt the need to get myself together. He chastised me on my shortcomings and encouraged me to do better with my life for myself and for my family. He expressed how I would be the primary role model to my son and how I was setting a poor example of being a man.

Hearing the truth hit a nerve. He was right, it was time to get myself together. Despite the hardships I faced in my childhood, I was both book smart and street smart. I wasn't a dummy, I just made a dumb decision to use drugs to escape my unhappiness.

After settling down from my high after that conversation, I choose to go job seeking. I went to a local fast food restaurant nearby to fill out an application.

While I sat in the dining area filling out the application, I felt motivated and enthused about getting my life and my family back!

That motivation switched lanes before I could complete the entire form. The urge to stimulate my drug addiction took over. So instead of completing the application, I wrote a note on the reverse side from where I wrote all my personal information: Name, date of birth, social security number, and previous work history.

I took the app to the manager at the counter, and she skimmed through it. She proceeded to tell me the hiring process. I told her to read the note I wrote on the backside. I put on an aggressive facial expression and slightly opened my jacket as if showing her a weapon underneath as she read the small note.

" I have a gun, give me all the money!!", it read.

She hurried to the register nearby, snatched all the cash from it and gave it to me. I ran out the door as fast as I could, headed straight to the dope man.

Since my personal information was enclosed on the robbery note, a warrant was issued out for my arrest. I stayed away from the area and was extra careful with breaking laws, trying not to get caught. I stayed in multiple local shelters and eventually ran out of options, so I moved to South Bend, IN with some relatives.

Instead of being somewhere out the spotlight of criminal activity, I got right in the middle of it. Several of my cousins were drug dealers and other relatives were drug users.

After been there on the run for a while, everything hit the fan. My cousins stopped serving[12] my uncle after pleading guilty to a drug case that was soon to be landing him in jail. He was a known user and under the radar with police, so my cousins didn't want to have anything to do with him and his drug usage. I wasn't fully aware of what was going on.

One day, my uncle asked if I could obtain some drugs for him from my cousin. They refused to sell to me once I told them it was for him.

My uncle was furious and went haywire! The police were

---

[12] Slang term used in lieu of selling

called and I ended up going to jail right along with my uncle.

The event made headlining news in South Bend Tribune. *"Wanted Milwaukee man **CAPTURED** by South Bend's Police Department."*

I was eventually expedited back to Milwaukee and sentenced to nineteen months of jail time.

For my final four months of incarceration, I was released to a halfway[13] house and enrolled in a drug treatment program. I was eager to start my new, sober existence.

I was instructed to report directly to the halfway house once I was released. Instead, I went straight to the dope house! Being clean during my incarceration time was simple because drugs weren't accessible. Now that they were accessible, using became my first priority.

I told myself I would take a few minutes to detour and get a small amount of drugs, it ultimately took a few hours. I came up with a plan of a bogus robbery attempt to justify not reporting to the halfway house right away as directed.

I had the guy I was getting high with punch me in the eye a few times to make it look more authentic. I ripped my shirt and rubbed dirt on me to add effects to my drama. His wife couldn't believe how vivid I made the robbery appear to be.

~ DEFINING MOMENT ~

This incident here was clearly a defining moment for me! I was a fiend[14] and I didn't even know it! I took drastic measures of

---

[13] Designated living facility for offenders on probation to be monitored when they have no stable living arrangement after prison release

[14] Fiend: A person who is excessively fond of or addicted to something

being intentionally battered to falsely justify my whereabouts to cover up my drug use.

As I entered the halfway house with my sob story, I realized it wasn't necessary. They knew my story was fake and they cared less to reprimand me for it.

This place was phony. The staff was only there for a paycheck and had no commitment to making sure the offenders maintained absolute sobriety or abide by the facility rules.

If I had known this before my "performance", I would have saved it for a later date.

Guys in there were getting high, including the night desk man who people paid to let them stay out after hours or to bring women into the facility.

About two weeks in, I went on a binge getting high. After a couple of days running the street, I turned myself in to my probation officer (P.O). I was incarcerated for a few weeks while waiting on a bed to open at another "treatment" halfway house.

Once released, I did pretty good in this place. I finally had my focus back. I had the mind that my life was back on track and I was going to make it. I had a job, was saving money, and I was looked at as an example to the other residents.

As I got closer to that 90th day, the "fear of success" started creeping in with the cravings to keep them at bay. One day, about two weeks from completing the ninety-day program, I quit my job. This was against the rules, so I was put on restriction for the duration of my stay. I was no longer allowed to leave the facility on a community pass as before.

The following Friday, I was allowed to leave to pick up my last work check. I told my counselor about my cravings and thoughts, that I needed him to send someone to go with me. I told him that I didn't trust myself. He told me he believed in me, the feeling would pass, I was stronger than that...everything I didn't need to hear! This was when the seed that treatment was a real farce was planted in my head.

I went and got my paycheck. I was nervous and scared. I really didn't want to use again. I quite a bit of positive self-talk on the city bus. On my way back to the center, the urge surfaced again.

The closer I got to the area of King Drive and Center Street where the check cashing place was, it got stronger and stronger. I tried to ignore it, but after getting the money in my hand, I couldn't make it to the drug house fast enough!

I ended up spending all my money, of course. I thought to myself that I would go back and get my money from the center. I arrived right at the moment the other residents were lined up to receive their weekly allowance from their accounts. I came in, the guys saw my appearance and sort of moved aside as I walked up to the office.

When I approached the desk to retrieve my finances, it was evident that I had relapsed. The counselor tried to reason with me, but I just wanted my money, not a rational reasoning.

It ended with me assuming I snatched my envelope after punching him. I took the monies of a few other residents as well. After running through all this money, I stayed at my girlfriend's house for about a week, then once again turned myself in to my P.O.

After two years of incarceration, I was released yet again. And, yet again, I went straight to the dope house. I told my P.O. I had somewhere to go so I wouldn't have to go to a halfway house, but I didn't have anywhere to go. I tried to game[15] my old

---

[15] GAME

girlfriend, but she wasn't having it. She was fed up with my repetitive ways of using drugs.

This rejection is typical during a struggle whether it's drug use or another addiction or habit. The ones you love wash their hands, turn their back on you or no longer want to associate themselves with you.

This was yet another *defining moment* as a fiend!

So, it was to the homeless trail I went. I spent the next few months between several well-known homeless shelters in the city.

The rejection from my ex-girlfriend aspired to do better. I got an old job back and eased up on the usage. It was an all-day, ongoing thing. I put lots of time into working. I was now what is referred to as a functioning addict.

One day I ran into one of my aunts and she told me I could stay with her. I met a few people in her building that got high, so it was a couple of months in serious using.

When I used, I escaped the realities I faced. One of those realities was the fact that my little cousin who was about twelve years old at the time, was in the house too. I knew that she understood my ways and I needed to escape the harsh reality that I was setting a poor example to her.

At this point in my life, I was tired of just existing. As soon as I got paid on Friday, I was broke[16] by Saturday morning. Plus, looking in the eyes of my little cousin, who looked at me without judgment, magnified the shame and guilt I had in myself. I knew I was better than this.

---

[16] Slang term meaning lack of money

One day on my way home from the store, I ran into my cousin's girlfriend, who had been a correction officer at the previous prison that my cousin and I was once in. <Still confused...Maybe we could remove the part of living with the co>We talked for a minute, and he told me how she was moving to Milwaukee for good. Long story short, I moved in with her to attempt to get myself together and took her offer to help me get on my feet.

I told her exactly what I was into, and how I had been living. She gave me a price for rent and told me no drugs in her house. I had every intention to do the right thing, but she lived in one of the city's notorious drug-filled areas, so it would be an immense struggle.

A guy I knew yelled my name from across the street one day while I was coming home from work. I went over and talked with him for a few minutes. Based on the familiar behaviors and obvious appearance of the guys he was with, I knew that they were on drugs and up to no good.

I went on my way, but as I was walking, that old nudge to get high came. I went home and fought the thoughts off. The next day after work, instead of going home, I went over on the block where a couple of my guys hung out. It wasn't long before I asked who had the best product and went to cop. After the first "morale booster[17], I was off to the races! It ended with me stealing some of my roommate's things and sold or exchanged them for drugs.

Another *defining moment* was stealing from my cousin's girlfriend who had done nothing but attempt to help me. Stealing and betraying the ones who love you is ordinary when your brain is tainted from drug use.

---

[17] The 1st high after not being high for some time; usually the first high of the day for frequent users

How ironic? The rejection comes from loved ones while betrayal comes from you.

Having no place to go, I found myself hanging out on the streets a couple days, then turning myself in. There was a warrant out for my arrest for not reporting as scheduled or absconding. I was fed up with my addition anyways the timing was perfect. It seemed as if the only time I could stay clean is when I was forced to stay clean without the access to drugs.

I ended up spending a few months in a correctional facility. Thankfully I didn't get my probationary period revoked. <I would've spent more time in a jail cell than in a treatment program.

My P.O. put me in another halfway house. I did what I usually did in this environment. I got a job, participated in the groups, became a role model, etc. But also like before, after that second work check, I used.

This place didn't kick you out after the first time. I was put on restriction and wasn't allowed to leave the premises. The next week though, I had to go get that last paycheck...yeah, I didn't make it back! At this time in Milwaukee, it was winter.

It was cold. I ended up spending hours at a spot[18] until the dope ran out.

Since it was cold, and I didn't have anywhere to go, I went and pulled my infamous job application scheme and robbed a local fast food restaurant. I went back and got high a couple more hours until I heard that familiar question, "What you about to do?" That simply meant it was time to leave. When the money to purchase more dope ran out, so did the hospitality!

---

[18] Spot- Street term for a drug house for dealers to make money while the users used in another room

So now I'm out in the cold with nowhere to go. I wander around trying to find a place to rest and get some kind of warmth. I tried doorways, cars, alleys, I couldn't find anywhere. After a couple hours went by, I ended up back by the restaurant where I pulled the earlier hustle at.

I noticed two police cars in the parking lot of a store about a block away. I walked over to them and told them I robbed the place up the street. The officers looked at each other and then back at me. They hesitated a moment before replying, most likely due to the fact that criminals typically don't tell on themselves.

One of the officers put me in the back of his paddy wagon while the other went to check to check out my story. He came back a few minutes later and   told the other officer that I was telling the truth.

To jail I went! I could care less about being locked in a jail cell and my freedom taken away. At that very moment, all I cared about was being out of the cold.

After three long years, the cycle continued after being released.

I isolated myself and sobered up and did a self-evaluation. This was it. I could no longer live my life this way. In and out of jail, not able to maintain sobriety every time I'm released. Not only did I lose everything and everyone I ever loved, I was risking losing myself!

The State of Wisconsin imposed a "Three Strikes Law". This law basically implied that repeat, persistent offenders such as myself could ultimately be sentenced to life imprisonment without the possibility of parole or extended supervision. I was already a three-time offender, so I didn't want to play roulette with my life by committing more crimes and going to prison. So, I basically took my life in my own hands and make strides to live a clean crime free life until I met a woman. I moved in with her after only seeing her a few times because I didn't want to be in Temporary Living Placement (TLP).

She was into all sorts of things, boosting[19], selling prescription pills illegally- various illegal angles to make money. She was on methadone for her addiction to heroine. I worked and since I didn't do pills or heroine, I felt that I was less prone to relapse.

Things started off great. We connected on so many levels and overall, we had a fair relationship to have recently gotten involved. We had our differences but the good outweighed the bad.

Life was treating me good at this point. I was clean, working a fairly paying job, in a stable relationship and best of all, I had my family back in my life. I was building the relationship with my son I always wanted, and I engaged more with my family and valued the time spent after missing so much over the years.

It all came to a head some months later when my girlfriend began saying I was choosing my son and my younger sister over her kids. No matter how I tried to reason with her and collectively engage all the kids in what I did, it just wasn't enough.

With all the tension going on in my relationship, I gained the desire to relieve some stress by resorting back to drug use. It was a temporary fix to get rid of my problems.

This started a week long binge!

Once I went back home, I packed my belongings and told my girlfriend that I was going to leave her. There was little hope for our relationship. I told her I planned on leaving when we

---

[19] Boosting: The act of stealing goods and sell to make a profit

returned from taking my son, my sister, and her daughter home to Southern, Illinois & Chicago.

When we returned to from dropping them off, the first thing she asked was if I wanted to stop and grab some drugs.

I was astonished because I knew that she didn't condone my drug use and had a zero tolerance for it. Not she went as far as using with me!

Now that I began to smoke regularly again, my girlfriend would make snide remarks about "crack-heads" and "dope fiends" trying to belittle me. But as soon as I talked about leaving her, she'd calm down and persuade me to stay with her. She even started lacing cigarettes and weed with cocaine to keep me from leaving her.

My job let me ago after I missed a mandatory shift without a valid excuse. I went to a temporary staffing company right away and I was going to start a new job the following Monday. Friday when I picked up my last paycheck, I spent it without including my girlfriend on the drugs I purchased.

Since I excluded her, she was upset with me and wouldn't allow me to drive her vehicle. After spending the money, I got another bright idea to go pull a quick robbery. Well, it didn't turn out so well. I ended up almost being beat to death and locked up facing life plus thirty years for my fourth robbery related offense.

Discussion Questions

Reflect back during the peak of your drug usage. Discuss the ruthless, unhealthy, damaging and regretful moments during those times.

1. What was your defining moment or lowest point during your addiction?
2. What were some of the most shameful things you did to supply your usage?
3. Who did you hurt, lie to, cheat or neglect during your using?

_____
_____
_____
_____
_____
_____
_____
_____
_____
_____
_____
_____
_____
_____
_____
_____
_____
_____
_____
_____
_____
_____
_____
_____
_____

Zachary Mitchell

Relapse

I've had quite a few relapses throughout the years. My first three incarceration periods were celebrated after release by getting high the first day out. For the first round of "forced sobriety" I did nineteen months.

The second period was for two years, and the third was three years. Between both the first and second, and the second and third, I had a few months in between where I was in treatment, halfway houses and a correctional facility waiting on these places, so I don't really consider these times as "legitimate" relapses.

Before being released after my third period of incarceration, the State of Wisconsin imposed the "Truth in Sentencing Law", which imposed severe on prison sentences, especially with repeat offenders.

The "new & improved" parole time was even stricter. So on top of all the enhancements, including the law key three strikes law, this new legislation had people spooked, including me.

I made a promise to myself that this time, I was not getting out of jail and going back to the same thing. But as usual, I ended up doing the same thing!

I was incarcerated from 2001 to 2008. This was my longest bid thus far. At the beginning of this time, I became a follower of Jesus Christ. I spent my time learning of my faith, that faith (being challenged regularly). I told myself that when I got out, crack was a thing of the past!

Everything was set up for me as I was preparing to face life on the bricks again. Before getting out, I enrolled in the Salvation Army's prison aftercare network. They connected with a mentor, who was and still is my pastor to date.

They provided me with a secured apartment at Hope Street Ministry which is a faith-based sober living residential facility.

I was released with several other guys who were under the same program. They met us as the bus station and took us to lunch and off we went to start our new life. The hospitality and kindness has always been present.

About two weeks later, I became involved with a woman. On the surface, she seemed to have it together, but it soon was revealed that she was not who I expected or anticipated her to be.

She was both a dealer and user of illegal prescription pills. They had her going crazy, so I ended the relationship quickly. I felt guilty because this is not how I wanted my first relationship encounter to be. I truly wanted to this woman to one day be my wife and not just a

During these first months out, I must say, I was tempted and enticed to get high, but I really was focused and used my support team. The only area I didn't was in the area of women. So about a week after ending it with the first lady, I got involved with another woman in April of 2009...she became my wife.

I was not prepared for marriage! But I believed she was "the one". She may have been, but we started of wrong! But I got heavily involved in ministry, I got a temp job at Quad Graphics, and at the same time went to school to be licensed with my SAC-IT.

I got the first part of my life story published and after finishing school, I got a job as a youth counselor at a group home. And when that ended, I was hired as an assistant community center director with the Salvation Army Citadel. God was really blessing me despite all my failure.

In the public eye, I was very busy and involved in a lot of good work, making a difference in the community etc., but at home, was different story. Me and my wife never really got on "one accord". It was chaos. There were times we had good times, but things just never got to the point to where we became "one". I take the brunt of responsibility for this.

So, in May of 2012, we separated, which led to divorce. I end up moving out and going to a men's shelter. Now that I have all this free time, I now start thinking "I'm free"! instead of needing to seek support during this time, I start running the streets before work, checking out old hoods I used to be in.

I start conversing with the women "out there" to see who was working. There was one woman that hung around the neighborhood the shelter was in. I know what she was about, and I got it in my head that I wanted to help her, but deep down, I just wanted to get with her.

I just didn't want anyone else in my business. To make a long story short, I ended up getting an apartment, went and found her and brought her to my apartment. She had drugs and said she needed to "get in the mood". I watched and then accepted the invitation. Since then I've had 4 other relapses.

After that first one, I did a ten-week outpatient treatment. A few months after completing that I fell again and had to do the four-month program at MSDF after completing that a few months later I fell again.

My job granted a ninety day leave of absence which I went the Salvation Army Adult Rehabilitation Center. After leaving there a few months later I fell again.

I went back to the ARC to complete the whole 6 months. A few days before graduation, they kicked me out for getting a job I didn't have permission to have. I left and went back to my apartment my landlord saved for me and went back to work.

Almost 2 months later, I fell again! For 3 weekends straight, I would pay bills then use. Each time was worse than the last. I told myself that was it... I quit my job, left my apartment and called my P.O. to sanction me til I could get my head straight. She suggested the sixty-day Relapse Prevention Program, which I'm glad I did, this finally tied some loose ends to my thinking of support groups "outside" of church activity.

Discussion Questions

Being sober is like conquering the world! But all it takes is one bad thought, experience or even a feeling, and it's back to the gutter.

1. What are some feelings that caused you to resort back to drug use?
2. What are some experiences you faced in which you found yourself back to using as a result?
3. What alternative actions did you take when facing the feelings or experiences noted above? Why did they fail? Or, was drug use your first alternative?

_____
_____
_____
_____
_____
_____
_____
_____
_____
_____
_____
_____
_____
_____
_____
_____
_____
_____
_____
_____
_____
_____
_____
_____

The "Hair" Trigger

In treatment and recovery programs, it is commonly advised to beware of certain people, places, and things. There are numerous strands of "hair" that can trigger a relapse.

Many facilitators recommend for a recovery addict not to get into a serious romantic relationship right away. They say you should wait until a year or two into recovery. But we rarely hear that we should abstain from sex itself for a while after leaving treatment.

Why would I say such a thing? I know eyebrows raised and mouths opened... I can't do that!... Ok check out this scenario...

Robert has just completed a 6 month in patient AODA treatment program. He gets out tomorrow. He is hyped, excited to get back out and travel the road to recovery. This is his fourth treatment in the past five years. It's time to finally get things together in his life.

Thankfully there are still a few people in his corner for support. He has a sponsor/accountability partner, a support group to go to, and a safe place to live. The next day he's released, and his sponsor picks him up to go for a celebratory lunch. They talk about his plan again, set up a time to meet later.

Robert runs some errands as his sponsor drops him off. They both joke about having 6 months of "pent up" energy that needs to be released and maybe he will meet someone soon... but no relationship for quite a while.

After leaving the community agency to work on getting some assistance, he walks across the street to the store for a juice or Gatorade. As he's coming out, he spots a woman across the street by the bus stop.

She makes eye contact with him and gives that knowing nod and smile. He thinks "let me go see what's up, I got 10 or 20 bucks to go head and get this frustration off, I'm not getting high, just have this quickie and it on to the apartment from there".

He goes and talks to her. He asks if she has a place they can go really quick, yeah... He'll give her 20 bucks. They get to an apartment, go to a back room. She gets him excited and says; "hold on a minute let me take a hit real quick so I can treat you real good!"

Robert is standing there with his pants down watching her take that blast, she looks up with smoke with smoke in her mouth and motions if he wants a "shot gun" ... she reads his mind!

Have you been in this situation? I have a few times. The intent was to just go have a quick sex session to relieve the horniness, and ended up as a relapse. And ladies can't say this scenario would work in your cases, but what about something like this...

Shelly has just completed the 10-week outpatient AODA treatment program. Her probation officer also helps her with getting her parenting classes so she could uphold the judge's order, so she could regain custody of her 2 young children. She's staying with her sister and sister's boyfriend, since they bailed her out of jail for attempted fraud.

These past few months have been a strain on her because she, once again, almost ruined her chances of regaining custody of her kids again. She hates supervised meetings with them and the way the social worker talks to them as if they were nuisances.

She willed herself to cut out all distractions on to concentrate on her sobriety. She has to go see her P.O. and on her bus ride home, she thinks to herself; "I wish I had a boo-thang to celebrate with. She hadn't had her itch scratched for quite a while and now she's itching bad!

Her phone rings and her sister were on the line saying "girl guess who just popped up out of nowhere? Lil Mike your crush from 2 years ago and he's on his way to see you" ....

She gets to her sister's house and Lil Mike is looking good and thinks to herself that her itch will finally get scratched. They go to her room and she's primed and ready... He says; "hold on, let me take this blow so I can treat you right... you still down?"

The situation may be a little more complex for women than men, but I do believe if we will admit it to ourselves that sex the act itself can be a deceptive trigger, we just don't see it as that because for the most part, we're given the image of different substances "enhancing" and making sex better. The beer commercials with the party scenes and the man and woman hook up. The most interesting man in the world

I heard of a sponsor from a AA group telling them not to get involved in serious relationships, but rather to hook up with random people and never see them again. In a perfect would that might work, but I believe just like having a beer or a drink can relax a serious crack or heroin addict back to his/her drug of choice...in the right situation... so can sex....

Discussion Questions

1. Has sex played a major role in your addiction? If so, how?
2. Do you believe that sex is truly a trigger to drug usage?
3. After experiencing intercourse while under the influence, do you believe it's possible to have good sex without drugs or alcohol?
4. Have you ever tried to be celibate? If so, how did it work for you? If not, why?

_____
_____
_____
_____
_____
_____
_____
_____
_____
_____
_____
_____
_____
_____
_____
_____
_____
_____
_____
_____
_____
_____
_____
_____

The End: Defeating

I mentioned that the sixty-day relapse prevention helped tie some loose ends in my outlook on recovery. There were three distinctive projects that really stuck with me.

There was a video by Delbert Boone titled, "The Predator", an autobiography by William "Cope" Moyers titled, "Broken", and a video titled, "Anonymous People".

The last video was awesome! It put a new, revolutionary spin to the A.A., N.A. rule of anonymity. Instead of being ashamed of telling your story and history with addiction, share it...outside of the group!

We don't have to be defined by public opinion as it relates to addiction. If we are to "recover", we can't hide it, we should share our story. Now we don't share other's stories, but ours is fair game!

Now don't think the temptation to use (or participate) won't be there...it will, no matter how many years you've been clean. The key, at least in my opinion, is to not think too far ahead. Take things one day at a time.

Find what helps you in your recovery, this isn't a "cookie cutter" walk, what may work for one may not work for another. As for myself, I believe it starts with coming into a relationship with our creator, Jesus Christ and coming into the family of Faith...at the same time staying connected with individuals who've been down the same road as I have in recovery.

But like I said, everyone must choose what works for them, and you must "do" something, it takes work to abstain! Keep phone numbers handy, use them.

Find a way to be involved with "giving back" to the community. It is so rewarding, and gives you a sense of purpose after so long of feeling worthless!

Discussion Questions

Take a moment to think about how blessed you are to have had others come to your aid and care about you being sober.

1. How important to your recovery is having a support system?
2. What does a healthy support system look like?
3. Where do you go for resources or treatment options?
4. Who can you trust to hold you accountable in your recovery?

_____

_____

_____

_____

_____

_____

_____

_____

_____

_____

_____

_____

_____

_____

_____

_____

_____

_____

_____

_____

_____

_____

_____

_____

_____

_____

_____

This portion of the book has been edited in spelling, grammar and punctuation. The content has not been altered or changed. These are actual thoughts written in the journal of Zachary Mitchell.

The Battle by Zac Mitchell

This book was due to be released quite about one year ago. I thank God for an understanding and supportive publisher to allow me to handle some personal issues that sort of hit me like a Mack truck.

Considering the overall theme of this publication, I think that it's vital that I be transparent and share something with you all. I'm conscious knowing that someone struggling with addition can have the growth, stretching, and victory by letting my story be a springboard in their own recovery.

Two days before Thanksgiving 2015, I got out of a 60-day in-patient treatment program. I moved into a "clean living" apartment complex. I wanted to try an N.A. (Narcotics Anonymous) group for support. I continued to attend my biblical groups for that spiritual guidance.

I attended one a few blocks from where I lived. I knew quite a few of the individuals there, so I didn't have that awkward feeling, but I just couldn't get with it. After a few meetings, I stopped going. When I stopped, someone told me about "Celebrate Recovery", a biblically based recovery group, but my schedule seemed to always conflict with the time of their meetings, so I never made it. But it is wild how all this ended up, but let me not get ahead of myself.

I started a new job a short time later. Things started to look good, at least on the outside. I reunited with a family member I hadn't seen in quite a few years. I'd go over her house and have lunch with her just chop it up.

She was on a fixed income, so I would supply her beer and the peach-flavored liquor that she liked. Eventually, I started to have a "little sip" with her every now and then, but never enough to get me to inebriated.

One day we were talking about the activities of her day and some things that transpired in the building she lived in. But in telling me, she basically admitted that sparingly, she still gets high! Now this was one of my past "get high" buddies and from what I knew, she was clean just like I was.

When I left her house, the conflicting thoughts started. Option one: "You know you need to cut that off! You're doing well, talk to someone, you WILL lose!". Then there it was option number two, "You can just dib and dab on the weekend or on your day off, plus she needs your help. You need something to relax from working so hard!" And just like that, I went with option number two.

So, the "double life" began, once again. I still went to my studies and even confessed to a few what I was doing. I had every intention to stop, but the hooks were in. These "hooks" were the set-up situations that were in place. Being offended, thinking others were trying to "be in my business", thinking I had everything under control. But slowly things started slipping away, just like they always had.

I began missing studies, slacking on my rent and eventually started missing work. It got to the point, after a couple months, people started to notice, especially those in my apartment complex. I was off my normal routine around there (basically I was in and out because I was trying to avoid being drug tested).

The week before the end, I was exposed to my church in such a way. I was out on a "run" on a Friday and ended up down the street from the building we hold our services in. I ran out of money, so I traded my car for more drugs. Basically, I rented it out in exchange for drugs from my dealer.

Once the drugs ran out, I extended the time for more. The dealer hadn't come back when he was supposed to, and it was getting late. My phone died, and I began to panic, not knowing if he would be returning my car. I used this pastor's cell phone who I saw down the street and he didn't answer.

I sat out there and just waited. A couple members from my church walked by and asked what I was doing over there, it was odd, because I was just sitting there. I went to the building where service was being held and used the phone.

More looks and questions, especially after I said someone had my car and wouldn't bring it back. People weren't naïve, they knew it meant that I bargained my vehicle for drugs. I walked around all night and eventually my car was returned on Saturday morning.

Well, I got home, out the streets and was on my grind[20] the whole week. When payday came, I had no intention of repeating what had happened the weekend before, I was exposed enough right? Wrong!

---

[20] Grind: Street term meaning make money or work hard

Friday, I had to work third shift so I spent most of the day getting high. I got myself together enough to sufficiently work my full shift but Saturday morning, I was back at it. I was scheduled to work second shift. I tried to find a replacement but couldn't.

I still had more dope, so I went to work and began using while I was there. The urge to leave got so strong that I left without making it half way through my shift. Spent my entire check on drugs and did the same thing with my car.

I walked around all night in a park smoking like I had a death wish. When it was over, walked almost three miles to get home. I slept the rest of Sunday away. Early Monday morning I checked on my car and he offered to extend the deal, so the next day and a half I was back to the races.

Ultimately, I ended up across the street from the church where the Celebrate Recovery group was. I had been meaning to attend the program many times.

I had a couple dollars left so I got some liquor and sat there drinking in deep thought. Suddenly, my mind snapped.

I started cursing myself out, those I thought were talking about me, the people that were misusing me, my church members, the drug dealer, everybody! I was having a dialog with a being I know to be a familiar spirit called suicide.

I text messaged quite a few individuals my thoughts and intentions. Some reached out and called me directly. My phone began to die so I'd power my phone on and off to check the time and reply to text messages. Luckily my friend Annie got ahold of me in between me trying to conserve power.

I trusted her to talk with me and help me out this situation. I went to her house for a while until we found somewhere I could go get help. I was admitted in a local hospital's psych ward for a few days to get myself together.

So now, I'm back in treatment. I want all of those fighting addiction to use my experience as "what not to do". I went through it for one of three reasons: 1) so you wouldn't have to, 2) so you'll know what NOT to do, or 3) so you can see you can make it!!

I want to encourage any and everyone to be on guard for the thoughts of "I got this". I've come to realize that when you think you got it, that's the very moment it has you! Let's not make this an everlasting battle! We can conquer and be victorious over this **battle** named addiction. Grace and peace to all!

I can do all things through Christ which strengthens me.

-Philippians 4:13

Exposed Roots Treated

Intro

Yep... once again! I go to help at a community outreach event on New Year's Eve. I'm feeling good, people are coming through, being fed, taking advantage of the resources we have available, everything. But what wasn't happening was me letting someone know that I was having thoughts of using!

I shrugged them off and told myself I wasn't going there, and the thoughts did subside... at least for a week. I was supposed to get myself into counseling after the last fall a few months prior, but I procrastinated.

A couple weeks after the new year, I used. Early that day I was feeling lonely. Once again instead of talking with someone or doing something constructive, I battled it myself.

Later that night I got a call that my nieces and nephews needed something to eat. Since it was late at night, I had already told myself that I wasn't going back out past 9pm. I told myself that I'd dropped the food off and go right back home, NO DETOURING!

On my way home, I got a glimpse of a woman standing on the bus stop. I rolled around the block, came back and offered her a ride. I spent the next couple weeks slipping and sliding, dipping and dodging getting high.

This led to my seventh time in a program, third inside a prison, all within the past five years. On the surface this looks bad, and it is considering the nature. But as I look at it now, the number seven means "completeness". I must say during this last period of treatment, some roots I thought were treated and done away with, were not.

What you'll read next will be some of the pieces of a reflective journal I kept while away. I wrote them pertaining to the personalized treatment plan, after finding out that the roots I thought were treated weren't. I even discovered a couple that were hidden.

In my treatment plan, I was given pamphlets directed towards a particular topic to aid me with sobriety as well as other traumatic issues rooted on the inside. With each topic, I wrote a reflective on what I get and take away from the topic and how it applies to my house. And again, I've decided to be transparent and share my thoughts *with my readers.*

There won't be any discussion questions to follow. This is just to let you all see into my personal "Discovering, Defining, and Defeating" recovery battle.

Low Self Esteem

Before reading this packet on Low Self Esteem, I would never have believed I had low self-esteem, not constantly that is. I believed everyone have their moments, but from the "dormant" explanation, I've had it quite awhile!

The lowest point I've ever been in my life was between 1997-1998. At this time, I was in heavy addiction. I was out on the "trail" (staying in shelters, eating in soup kitchens). I remember seriously thinking this would be my destiny in life, to be a dope-fiend[21].

As I kept going to prison, my thinking began to change. I started seeing I was more than just a dope-fiend. Being incarcerated forced me to remain sober and that was a big help. I was on the right track mentally.

I really thought I was cool once I became a believer in Christ! I've been to many treatment programs, NEVER has anyone hinted that I felt low about myself. Most, even my Pastor, says I have TOO MUCH pride, thinking too highly of myself! But I see now that by me wanting to appear to have it together all the time: not asking for help, the isolation, the "self-sabotaging", the over-eating, the constant relapsing, the wanting to

---

[21] A person heavily addicted to dope

fit in and be accepted, the self-criticism (which I defined as positive self-talk to get me in gear), all of these things had roots in low self-esteem!

I love how God work! I'm glad to have "connected the dots", as I've gotten myself here yet again. I see my early life influences really set me on a destructive course in life, but I made it through to this day. I don't believe in coincidence, He says the spirit will lead us to "all truth", I'm glad to know the truth of me, now I can fight a better fight.

Trust

When I think back, I believe my trust/distrust issues started when I found out that the man I grew up believing was my father, really wasn't at the age of fifteen. I was mentally and emotionally disturbed by that revelation. I could remember the times growing up, prior to find out, my cousins would tease me saying he wasn't my father. I'd go ask about it and was told, "Boy get out of here! Don't listen to that mess."

The things that were said and done to me all became clear, I wasn't his! Up until that point, I thought he was doing what all "fathers" did. When I found he wasn't, my trust was affected immediately!

Growing up, I had a soft spot for the kids who no one would play with, you know, the outcasts. If kids teased another for having an odor, not dressing in the latest fads, and ostracized them, I would befriend them. I never liked nor could respect a bully, not matter how popular they were.

But these qualities were pushed to the background at age fifteen. In fact, I came to believe these qualities were "sucker" qualities. People would use these against you, look at what happened to me! Even though I wasn't the cause of it, so much had happened.

Eventually I started the "I'm going to get you before you get me" type of lifestyle. I really didn't know who I was at this point or where I fit in. If he wasn't my pops, then they really weren't my family, so who was I?

From this point of view, I became a chameleon, trying to blend in different groups. Sometimes others would make fun of me or I would feel self-conscious, so I started using them to get what I wanted. This lasted many years. At the same time, it made people not trust me and caused them to draw away from me as well.

Emotional Blackmail

Coming up, I experienced emotional blackmail in different ways. The most prevalent method was by the "punisher". I was always on edge out of fear for any type of discipline, whether physical or non-physical.

As I relate it to the relationships I've had, I was the "punisher" in my first marriage. I was also a little of the "tantalizer" because of where I was in my life at this time. I needed a sense of control. She gave me an edge when two things happened. 1) She asked me if she should loan an aunt some money, whatever I told her to do, she would do it. 2) I went off[22] on her in front of her family when an old boyfriend of hers came by her grandmother's house while we were there. I got angry and I left.

She came home not long after asking him to leave and apologized to me. Everything went good for a while, but when drugs entered the picture, she "woke up" and was out of there.

In my second marriage, I was the "punisher" and the silent type of guy. If she didn't do what I liked or wouldn't act on my suggestions, I would blackmail her by not doing normal activities, wouldn't go places and for the most part, I'd just

---

[22] To snap out, yell at or curse out

shut down.

I knew these emotional blackmail situations were out of line. However, after growing up emotionally unattached, this was my withdraw method. Truly shows how childhood or old experiences sets a precedent in how we respond in situations today.

Valuing Yourself & Others

It's wild how all this works. On one hand I consider myself to be a sane, functioning adult male. I do my best to treat others how I want to be treated, I help others out when I can, I empathize with others, I have confidence that I can and will succeed in life, etc. But at the same time, I can second guess myself, care what others think about me, overthink and read too much into things.

For a long time, I equated this as just being human. Some days will be better than others, but never did I think it had to do with having low self-esteem. Even in my worst of times, I felt somewhat good about myself.

I've really been digging within to put the pieces together between what I call the mind traps that were instilled when I was younger to my recent troubles.

There was a book titled "House of Healing: A Prisoner's Guide to Inner Power and Freedom" by Robin Casarjian that was given to the inmates in in-patient treatment. There was a chapter that talked about having a conversation with your "inner child". No, I won't have a conversation with him, I thought to myself. I can't, he's grown now!

But what I will do is look in the mirror and tell him that he made it through it all, tell him that he *survived! After going through so much physically, mentally and emotionally, it was conquered! Now that's something to put value in, definitely worth to share the "wealth" with someone else!*

Addicted to Unhappiness

Although I don't agree with most of the child rearing advice provided in this pamphlet or during the discussion of the topic, I did glean some good insight from it. As I read, I thought about my own upbringing and how my pops set those mental roadblocks.

Such as the times I had to give up my toys to my younger brother a week or so after Christmas Or, allowing me start things (the tenor sax, basketball at school, boy scouts, etc.) without finishing. It seemed as if, once he saw I was really interested, he would force me to quit.

Then there were times when he'd make me look for things and tell me that if I didn't find it in a certain amount of time, I would get a whooping.

As they explained how different events from childhood could affect your adult life, I started to see the correlation. The testimonials really tied this up for me. I can see now why it seems every time I get to a certain place in life, I subconsciously go to the left or fall short.

One situation from my childhood that stood out was when we moved from Santa Clara, CA. to Morgan Hill, not that far away. We moved to Morgan Hill from the shelter we were staying in. in middle of basketball season. I was on the team and Morgan Hill was in the same division.

When I transferred from Santa Clara, I couldn't get on the team because it was too late in the season. The coach took a liking to my skills from a few pickup games I played against him in. He said he could help me get to college after high school. He talked to my mom and pops, told them I had talent and that he wanted to help me. He even offered to allow me to stay with him and his family.

Pops told him he would think about it. He asked me if I wanted to and I told him that I did. He acted as if he was distressed from my decision and turned around and told the coach no. he used the excuse that we were moving back east. I was heated[23]! But these incidents, I see, may have a big impact on me not getting "over the hump" in life. It was if I couldn't win for losing so to say

Then there's the relationship issue. My mother didn't really spend much time or show me much affection growing up. We spent much more time with grandmother than with our own mother.

When my mother and pops would have arguments, she'd just up and leave and would move back here to Milwaukee. I'm the oldest, so I spent a lot of time raising my younger siblings until I was about fifteen to sixteen, then I was in

---

[23] Upset

California and southern Illinois until I was eighteen.

At different stages growing up, I saw mom in different situations. Pops introduced her to drugs back in the day and she ran with it. When I returned to Milwaukee after they left CA for good, she was in bad shape. My siblings needed care. I think seeing the situation she was in, strung out and addicted to drugs, I saw the "cycle" continuing and I resented her.

My first wife couldn't understand why I started using after we were married. She knew about my upbringing. She once said I acted like I hated her (it was really myself I was mad at because I didn't know what I was doing). Then years later my second wife said I didn't trust women, and later, another woman I dated said the same thing. These trust issues led to what I consider an addiction to unhappiness. And it all stemmed from the distrust and resentment I felt against the first woman in my life, my mother.

There was part that talked about setbacks, that we need to be aware of when things are going good in some areas, but we need to also be aware of things going awry in others. It could be that "slippery slope" on the horizon, that was real. All in all, this book was insightful with a lot of meat or substance in it.

Overcoming the Real Pain of a False

I believe the key for healing from a "false self" doesn't come from self, in my case, from me. The false self was created and conditioned because of how I perceived the "lessons" of parents, teachers, society, etc. I had all these examples of what love was or wasn't.

But all these "influences" had influences. Then there's the commonality that crosses race and culture borders. I believe that you must come to the end of yourself, as I did in 2001, and come to grips with the reality that "truth" is a BEING. So is the LIE and we make our choices based off their suggestions.

For me to truly and finally overcome what I've experienced these past few years is to believe my false self has no life in him. I must keep my mind focused on the TRUTH, not A truth, or it will always appear that I'm just an actor on a stage. There is a natural mirror I look at to see what I look like, the same is true spiritually.

Ways of Coping After Trauma

My main way of coping, especially these past few years, has been to withdraw from others. I believed this was the best way to deal with the problems "I" created and didn't want to involve others, even though I knew that isolation wasn't the way to do it. Guilt, shame and all that comes with being exposed made that the best option in my mind.

If I was having a bad day at work or having difficulties with other individuals, I would do a variety of things to get through it. I'd simply talk to someone else, listen to music, take a walk, pray, think it through, count to ten, etc. But when it came to the temptation and struggle to use and relapse, I did nothing but isolate myself.

It's not like I don't know effective, more healthy ways to cope. I do have networks of supportive people and relationships that are healthy to draw to, I just need to utilize them. I need to solidify in my mind "now" what I will do and who will be my "go to" person no matter what. I need to stay away from anything that resembles the "mindfulness" technique, being in my own mind is my greatest obstacle!

Reversing Our Core Beliefs

I believe the belief that is the most imbedded in my life is the one that says "I" must make sure I'm good. And that if I rely on others or let anyone else too close, they will take advantage.

The problem with this in my life now is that I say I don't think this way anymore (I don't) and I'm not living this way, consistently, anymore. Yet for the last five years I've isolated and self-destructed numerous of times! So, either I will continue to be a walking contradiction or roll up my sleeves and do some digging.

To challenge and reverse this belief I will, I MUST, confront this belief head on. Instead of sizing people up or questioning their motives, I will take them at their word, especially if they show genuine concern. I won't overthink their questions and let them know when I'm going through, especially if I say they are a part of my support network.

I do believe we were created for fellowship with others...we are to appreciate the fact that although we're all different...we're all the same. It's time for me to finally shatter the illusion that I'm an island unto myself.

Thinking Things Through

The most traumatic event and the most life changing event, happened within four days of one another back in 2012. Before this, there was no processing thoughts or caring about other's feelings where my beliefs were concerned. Either you respected and accepted them, or you moved around. My thinking was just that...mine.

After the life changing event, all my beliefs were challenged and started to change. Things were going well until late in 2008. This is when someone came into my life and all those beliefs came back like a flood. But instead of checking them "consistently" against my new set of beliefs, I allowed myself to drift back into the comfort of that trap.

So now here I am, going through the process once again, separating the old from the new. This is more challenging and difficult for me because I don't, in my inner being, live by the same beliefs I once did. But, being here at this time says something to the contrary.

I guess the process will be valuable to me because it gives me an alternative to the "new normal" I've been living in these past few years, which has been confusing to everyone, including myself.

Learning to let go of the Illusion of Control

As far as my family stepping in and trying to control my using/non-using, that has been non-existent. The closest I've seen to this is my younger siblings trying to "fuss and joke" it out of our mother. My baby sister, awhile back, made a comment that maybe I needed to move away and join them.

My church family and friends tried the first couple times, my bosses at different jobs, but they got fed up with it and now it's like they're saying, "We've tried, you're not gettin it, we'll wait to see what you're going to do!"

I've tried to control it, monitor it, excuse it, refuse it...it doesn't work! The best thing for me to do is to do the work and abstain from it. I can control the hate I have for it and what it has done to my life.

Trauma

The trauma I've experienced happened mostly early in life. As a child I was physically and emotionally abused. Physically I say because quite a few times the whooping was too severe for the action or over and above the "time limit". Emotionally I was abused because there was always the "threat" of something, the name calling, put downs, etc. Two male figures sexually abused me (this memory resurfaced later in life). I also saw my mother beat and a host of other emotionally traumatizing things as well.

Three different times in life, I could have died by strangulation. At age fifteen, my pops (who I just had found out wasn't my biological) and I had a fight. He got on top of me and dug into my throat for my windpipe. It was horrifying, and I truly thought that I was going to die.

In 2001, while some guys were restraining me for the police, one of them got his arm around my neck and choked me out. Before I blacked out from not being able to breathe, I thought, "I'm going to die like this." A few days after this, I had thoughts of hanging myself from the top tier at the county jail, I seriously contemplated it, and made the decision to do it, but was miraculously stopped.

In 2015, I was contemplating jumping off the 35th St. viaduct and in 2016 I considered jumping into the Lincoln Park pond.

I've been divorced twice and after the second, I relapsed after eleven sober years. How I "get through" is through my faith. But like anyone who truly cares for you, God will love you enough to decide to let you have what "you" choose!

What Does It Mean to Trust

It's easy for me to be upset and bothered by some individuals who "betrayed my trust" after all I did to show them how much they could trust me. Then the fog lifted!

It's wild, thinking it through now, how I can blind myself to some situations where others really needed me. I've promised to be there, but didn't come through, a few times even at the last minute! Yet despite being unreliable, people kept dealing with me.

But I couldn't have the decency to extend the same courtesy to them? When in all actuality, can I really expect them to put themselves in a situation "I" created?

I tend to give myself a pass on being untrustworthy, excusing it, even when I made a verbal contract, but want to put everyone else in the "you used me" category at the first thought of betrayal. When, really, after the smoke clears, it's not betrayal at all. It's just a "you need to get your act together" situation.

My trust issues, I believe, lie more or so with myself than with others. It's just I may not want to look in the mirror. Sometimes looking at another is a reflection, but it's still "on you".

Promiscuity

Me, promiscuous? I never would have thought this to be true. I thought this meant you were just running through women all the time. I've had my share, but there were times where I went periods of time between women, especially during prison bids.

As I really ponder and think about this, what about mentally? What about subconsciously? I was exposed to porn at a young age, which brought on masturbation. I've unwillingly conditioned my mind to have a skewed view of women. I don't go around just undressing and slamming women in my mind, but I did have the view that they all wanted sex and would do whatever to get it.

Growing up, it was nothing to pass women around in the family. If she was willing to "go", we encouraged it. A couple uncles ran havoc in one of my friend's family with his mom and daughter. Us cousins used to share girls and women as well.

I see now how even though I'm past that now and I don't mess with a lot of women now, I do still sometimes have a "roaming" mind. I've still struggled with porn. I still can be flirtatious. My last wife once said to me that she noticed I was a butt man, she saw how my eyes were wandering in public places.

I won't get into the height of the dope dating era! Yes...promiscuous all the way!

Going forward, I believe my biggest challenge in this area will be simply to guard my "eye gate". Porn has to be history and I have to look at women as the bible says, the older women as mothers, the younger as sisters. I will date, and I will focus all my attention on the one I'm with and put blinders on to the rest.

The Voice in my Head

It's wild how the two descriptions used in this packet were "guardian angel and fallen angel". My thoughts are totally in line with this rationale.

I believe the cartoons had it right when they sometimes showed an angel on one shoulder and a devil on the other. I believe that the spiritual realm dictates the natural one. I don't believe every "voice" in our head is our own. I believe like a company has a board of directors that may be for or against the direction of the company...so does life.

I didn't always have this clear understanding. In 2001 my mind was awakened to this knowledge. Before attempting my last armed robbery, I was thinking of pulling another "application" stunt as I did twice before for some quick money. When I went to the Burger King to do it, a young man met me at the door as they were about to open.

He was kind of rude and aggressive for some reason (I didn't know at the time that this was the last day this location would be open). I asked for an application and he told me they didn't have any. As I walked away, a little voice in the back of my head said, "Dude tried to treat you like a punk!" I audibly said "Yeah!" I looked around and found a metal pipe and went back to the restaurant to rob it. What did I do that for! I was beat and almost choked to death.

Four days later I was in the county jail and I felt that suicide would be the best solution to get me out of the predicament I was in. After going back and forth with the suicidal thoughts, I made the decision to do it after I went to sleep. Before I laid down, I heard another voice telling me to get a bible and read about Paul. When I woke up, this was all that was on my mind.

Now, I still had the choice to choose between those two. I'm glad I chose the second. Me sitting here shows me that this is a lifelong battle. I better get a deeper, fuller, clear understanding of the "tactics and motives" of the voices in my head. One is a "beautiful liar" who can dress chaos and distraction in a wonderful array of packages. He tries to make THE TRUTH seem as if he is restrictive, dangerous, or a myth.
I believe we all have three different voices going on interchangeably all the time in our heads. I need to constantly be aware of who I'm listening to.

Overcoming the 3 Stages of Substance Abuse Addiction Denial

Although I know I need to get involved in a support group and one on one therapy in the community, my failure and procrastination these past few years places me in stage two denial.

I believe I have an addiction to cocaine, but I don't believe my IDENTITY is "Zachary Mitchell the addict"! My idea of chemical dependency is that of someone like a diabetic who needs insulin to live. A counselor at the Salvation Army, ARC, once told us that you could set an ounce of weed, an 8 ball of cocaine, and a bottle of vodka on a dresser. He said neither one would move unless you go and pick one up. And if you don't pick up either, how can you abuse it? I can also see it from the rationale of when things get rough or I start experiencing certain feelings, I run back to "old faithful" to give me comfort as well.

This packet spoke a lot about the innermost being (spirit) aspect of all this. I think about the barrier that seems to rise that keeps me from getting plugged in out there, although I did schedule an appointment with a therapist a week before I came in here, I just didn't make it.

I think about a biblical reference to all this which makes sense to me. The Greek word for sorcery is "Pharmakeia" where the word pharmacy derives from. I believe in spiritual beings and their *influence, and how powerful those influences are, especially when you've practiced them for so long.*

I also believe in the power of choice and that I can choose the greater influence to give me the strength to get pass this "illusion" of peace and security and remember the "old man" has led me almost to death many times. So yes, stage two denial is where I sit at the moment.

Everything in life has a season. And in every season, there's different weather, different people and different situations that come from the changing of the temperature. There's sometimes where the temperature gets too hot or the temperature may get too cold. At this point in life, the temperature is just right.

I have a clear mind and clear understanding of my faults during the seasons that have been hindering my mental, spiritual and overall growth. I've been in position to reflect and dig deep into the impediments that may have gotten in the way of me getting to the root cause of my issues and habits.

As I stated in the introduction of this book, I've come to the realization that the roots of my childhood and early adulthood affected my life tremendously in relation to the continuous drug use. But I declare an end to it all as I start a new life and journey! And I touch and agree with anyone battling anything that hinders their growth- victory is yours!

"The Foster Theory"

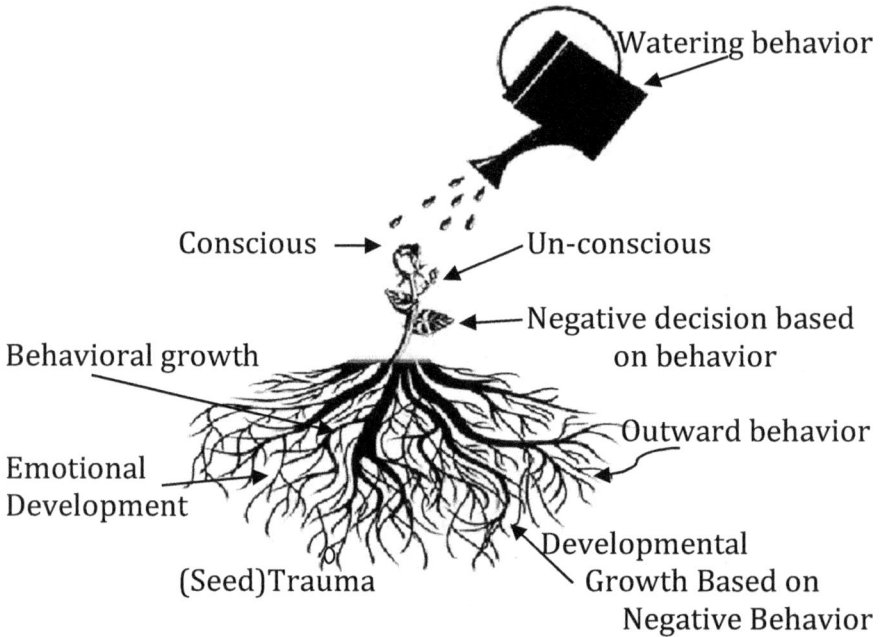

When you think about getting to the root of why you choose to run to whatever it is you use to escape or feel better, think of it as the watering of the plant that has grown from the seed of the trauma you've experienced. They may have been planted early in life, even in childhood. Sexual, mental, physical abuse, neglect, abandonment, divorce, job loss, depression, and many more.

The diagram above was created by my counselor, Mr. Foster. It brings a clinical revelation to life and provides visual to make it applicable to a being as a flower.

Watering behavior (the addiction or progressive recovery) determines whether you'll produce flowers that'll add beauty to the landscape of your life. Or the weeds that makes it unpleasant to look at and sucks the life out and deteriorates your floral structure.

A Message from the Publisher

Indestructible, durable, long-lasting, reinforced, tough, resistant, sturdy- all sums up, UNBREAKABLE! I would personally like to apply this alliance of adjectives to the men and women who've had the courage to defeat drug use!

The experiences you've endured during your addiction are unimaginable and not all beings are fit to sustain such strife!

If you are still struggling with addiction, just know that your end is here and it's time to declare your life, your family and sanity back!

God has chosen YOU to face trials and tribulations just to come out stronger than ever! There is no more living at the bottom of the barrel for you.

"For though the righteous fall seven times, they rise again, but the wicked stumble when calamity strikes." -Proverbs 24:16 (NIV)

Discover those things that tempt you, define the circumstance that puts you in position and defeat the fiend and addict in you.

-Clarissa Green Sole Proprietor

ABOUT THE AUTHOR

Zachary Mitchell was born in Milwaukee, WI. He spent a big part of his adolescent years in different parts of California, among other places. He went back to his origin, Milwaukee, permanently in 1989.

He has one son, one grandson, five nephews, and six nieces. He's a father figure to six additional children. He has three brothers and four sisters.

Zac, short for Zachary, is a man with an extensive history with addictions of all sorts. He's set his pride aside and has shared pieces of his story to help others gain victory in recovery.

His autobiography, "*My Road to Damascus Experience*", was written and published in 2009. This book highlighted his personal-life journey, emphasizing the fact that even the toughest roads could lead to God just like the apostle Paul in the bible.

Zac has come to the realization that treatment can be ineffective and misleading to some struggling with drug addiction. He decided to share his personal approach with hopes of it being an aid to others during their road to recovery by composing this book, '*The Fiend*'.

With the many life shortcomings, Zac has still been able to walk firmly with God by trusting and depending on His word, the Holy Bible.

Zac is an "urban missionary[24]" to the streets of Milwaukee, the same ones he contributed to the degradation of. His mission is to draw others to Christ, especially those who may not feel worthy to be at the forefront of His throne.

---

[24] A person who spreads the word of God amongst urban and impoverished areas

This book is available for purchase at the following:

Available at www.createspace.com/7586090
Available on Amazon.com
Available on Amazon Europe
Or contact the publisher at Unbreakable@yahoo.com

www.ingramcontent.com/pod-product-compliance
Lightning Source LLC
Chambersburg PA
CBHW062019040426
42447CB00010B/2070